Commanded to Homeschool

A Story of Freedom from Generational Bondage

Adrienne A. Brown

Commanded to Homeschool Copyright © 2018 by
Adrienne Brown
No part of this book may be reproduced or transmitted in any form or by any means, mechanical or electronic including photocopying or recording, or by an information storage and retrieval system, or transmitted e-mail without permission in writing from the publisher.
This book is for entertainment purposes only. The views expressed are those of the author alone.

Published by
Adrienne A. Brown
Orange,VA
www.Practicalmindedness.com

I wrote this book for all mothers who find themselves in a similar predicament with their children.

I also wrote this book for all the little children (especially boys) who find themselves being labeled hyperactive, incapable, and lacking inquisitiveness.

Lastly, I wrote some of my experiences down in hopes of helping someone else gain the confidence to break free of all labels and stereotypes.

Adrienne A. Brown

For Michael Brown, my husband.

Thank you for supporting me and protecting me while I was mothering our sons. Without your strong presence holding me up, I would not have been able to sustain this dream of being wife and mother.

Your steadfast leadership kept us safe, and secure.

In you I have learned what true love really means.

Commanded to Homeschool

Table of Contents

Mystery Lady 1

"Single Mom, Raising Two Boys" 13

Empowerment 28

Working With What I Had 43

Implementing in the Lives of My Sons What I Learned from
God's Word 55

Teach Them Your Actual Name or They Will Call You
Mommy 72

Utilizing the Henry Ford Tactic "Finding a Man or Woman in
Five Minutes" 78

Engaging My Community 100

Extra-Curricular Activities 109

Testing 133

Intentional Training 143

Middle School and More 170

High School Days 188

College 219

Mystery Lady

One morning, I was headed into a Safeway store in Woodbridge, Virginia, when I noticed a middle-aged white woman coming toward me. As I walked toward the store grasping the hands of my two young sons, she walked toward me, talking to me. "You know," she said, "you need to homeschool your sons." "They will not get a fair chance in this school district!" Now, as you can imagine,

I was quite taken aback. I didn't know this lady. What the heck was she talking about? Homeschool?

Now up to this point, the only person that I knew who was doing something like that was another young white woman from my neighborhood. Someone I would casually say good morning to as I played in the park with my boys. During these play times, we talked a little and I wondered why her children were not getting on the bus with the other neighborhood children. They were clearly of age. That's when she told me that she homeschooled the children. I remember thinking, "Oh, she must be a school teacher." But I learned that not only was she not a teacher, she struggled to pay for her books. She used the Abeka curriculum. She also told me that her father helped her to purchase the needed curriculum every year.

My conversation and thoughts about homeschooling had gone no further than that neighborhood playground. So, when this mystery woman from the Safeway parking lot came to me with this God ordained proclamation, I felt weirdly attracted to her words. I was compelled to think outside the box of what I had accepted as my boys sure future with the public school system. "Me, homeschool? I don't know the first thing about that," I protested. "Oh, yes, you do," she retorted. "I can't afford it," I argued.

Now, the conversation with this mystery lady caused me to finally think about the other conversations with my homeschooling neighbor. Suddenly, I was realizing why I never gave this idea a second thought after leaving that playground every morning. The mystery woman continued, with her persuasive words. "I know a family who is doing it on a shoe string budget," she said.

"But, I don't know how to teach! I can't keep my kids' home."

"You can, and it is your parental right to do so." She spoke with complete confidence to my right to homeschool, as well as, to my abilities to do so. Remember, I had never seen this lady before in my life. "I will give you all the information you will need to understand this school system. It will help you get started with homeschooling."

Then she reached into the bag that she was carrying and handed me a packet of papers. She gave me her business card and wrote names and phone numbers of some homeschooling families in my neighborhood.

Wow! As I am writing this, I am astonished as to how thorough God is.

As this mystery woman explained to me which person to contact first and how close they lived to me, my two boys were fidgeting a little, but stayed near. I didn't know what to do, or what to say.

The boys didn't appear to care one way or the other about our conversation. All though it was all about them and their educational futures. This strange woman was truly bothering me, yet I was drawn to her affirming words. So, I just accepted her papers, placed them in my purse and thanked her for the information.

"Alright, now, you be sure to contact those people, okay?" she demanded adamantly, nodding her head yes. Clinching the hands of my small sons, I smiled, said good-bye and went into Safeway.

I was in a fog about their education. I had no idea about any other method of schooling. It never crossed my mind to do anything else, and neither did I know that there was any other way to educate a child. I only knew that my boys would go to school, like all of the other minority children that I saw in my neighborhood.

Ah, that's it! That's what I realized, as this mystery woman spoke to me. I finally knew why I never gave any deep thought to my conversations with my homeschooling neighbor.

I wasn't supposed to think like "them" whites. I was to follow formalities just like all my other brothers and sisters of color, which I knew at the time. How could I ever think that I could homeschool?

I had so many things going against me, I thought. I was a minority. I couldn't be trusted to educate my sons as well as the school system. Besides, I had to quit school in my senior year, for the safety of my mother and grandmother. I didn't have a college education. I came from the "hood." Me, homeschool?

At the time, I was a single working mother, recently separated, and struggling to raise my sons to the best of my ability. I wasn't even from Virginia. I had no family in this area, just me and my two boys. Not to mention, I was a new Christian attending a church where I didn't really know anyone. I hardly even knew anything about the God I worshiped. This church was an all-black church, where most people appeared to be more educated, seemed to have more money, and were pro-public school.

One of my best friends was my next-door neighbor, who seemed to truly love the Lord. Who gently befriended me, despite my wavering ways. I knew her opinion about school. She often would say that she couldn't wait to put her children on the school bus. So how can I be expected to do something different? Plus, my ex-husband would never go for that idea. So that's why I emphasized that these women were white woman. Hoping that you would understand my initial reluctances to homeschool. I did not know one black or Hispanic person that homeschooled. None of my black co-workers did. I knew of no one in my immediate family, back home in San Francisco, that homeschooled. As far as I could see, none of the blacks from my apartment complex did. As I sat on that playground, talking with my white homeschooling neighbor, I watched all the children being escorted to the school bus, their mothers giddy with anticipation. My heart ached as I took in this scene, because I knew that next year that would be me, but I would not be happy to see my son go.

"Single Mom, Raising Two Boys"

"An entire year has gone by and my oldest son is ready to start kindergarten. I haven't trusted in my own ability to educate my son. I must work in order to live. My mind is numb; I am sickened by the thought of putting him on the bus. I just couldn't understand how the other mothers could be so relaxed about this decision. I found it extremely hard. I didn't want other people having such control over my son, especially for so many hours of the day. I want to go work at the school, but I have a three-year-old at home. Pulling him ever close to me, I pinned the bus shaped tag to my five-year old's shirt and walked him toward the bus stop. I was torn, torn to tears."

You're probably wondering what ever became of my encounter with the mystery woman in the Safeway parking lot. Well, my curiosity was peeked. She had persuaded me to call some of the people and talk to them about their current homeschooling. I called up one of the families. The father answered the phone. After explaining who I was, and who had given me his phone number, he was delighted to have me come over. I was truly stepping out on what little faith I had.

This man was very polite. Turns out he was the primary educator in the home. His wife had the better income earning potential, so they decided that he would stay home while she worked. I thought that was weird. Yet, I was dazzled by how they handled the school. He showed me the books that he used for math, language, reading. His family had even been featured in the major newspaper in an article about homeschooling. There were photos of his children doing school, sitting at the kitchen table, with books spread out. There were also photos of them learning about gardening, by actually working in the garden. I saw pictures of them and their mom in the kitchen, as she taught them how to cook. There were pictures of them walking through the grocery store with dad, using a shopping list that had been written by their mom.

As he took me on a tour of his home, I noticed the girl's walked with us. They were so eager to show us their daily routine. There was something very different about these children. They were of varied ages, old enough to be stand offish, indifferent toward me as an adult. Yet, they seemed completely comfortable, conversing with me.

They were completely at home with my children, looking and sounding like little educators themselves. I made a mental note of that in the back of my mind. It was unusual how they seemed so mature. Not in a nasty, stereotypical, young teen kind of way, but in a refreshingly composed matter of fact way. Their father helped me to see, just how easy and rewarding it would be for me to educate my children. Knowing that I was a single working mom, he suggested some possible alternatives to earning an income from my home as I homeschooled.

After many hours of exploring my possibilities, I left that family's house, full of new-found hope. I had been schooled. This was radical, innovative, freeing, self-empowering, all the above. Still, I filed this knowledge in the dungeon place of my mind's slothfulness.

I worked as a contractor for the Department of Defense, each year our contract went up for bid. It was always a waiting game, to see if the incumbent workers would retain their positions. While my position had been secured for most of the contractual changes, this particular year, which was prior to my son starting school, I had to take a pay cut. In addition, I was passed over for a position that I could perform backwards if needed. The job was given to someone that had a bachelor's degree in the medical field. This person knew nothing about computer inventory, which is what I did, yet they became my boss. So, my pay was cut, I was passed over, I had to train the person who got the position, and she became my boss.

That was as frustrating to me as it was helpful to jolt my brain into thinking toward being home. I pondered with the idea of being home with my boys, starting a daycare in my home, and homeschooling them. I used the rest of that year researching every avenue available to me. I didn't have a cell phone, I didn't have the internet, all I had was a land line. So, I called different agencies asking questions about business licensing, training, and regulations. Stressed out with work, taking my boys to daycare every day, doing everything alone, I couldn't deal with the demands of life anymore. I quit. I just stopped living the way that I was. It was eating me up, every time I had to leave my children. I would receive notes about my oldest son's "behavior" from the daycare workers. I felt as if he was being labeled somehow, and not yet aware of the ADHD track, I tried to adjust my son's character. I felt in my soul that I needed to do something different.

I could feel that my entire life style was soon to change. Although I still couldn't see my way to start homeschooling, I did start something. Using all the information I had gathered from various people and places, and remembering the encouragement from that homeschooling dad, I started a daycare in my apartment. Thank God, I lived in the kind of rentals that went by my income.

You guys let me tell you! That though I was walking through this time in my life, I was moving completely in the "little" Holy Ghost power that I knew. I really didn't have too much of a clue, as to what I was doing.

So, at first, everything seemed like it wasn't going to work out, I was feeling a little panicked. Then I started to get neighborhood children rapidly. This was due to the fact that I lived right next door to my best girlfriend, who was running a very successful daycare from her apartment. It is funny how God used her in so many ways to teach me about trusting Him. The knowledge I gained from her example was not only for my daycare.

It would be the very thing that would help me to know for certain about my child's academic capabilities, once he started school. My girlfriend gave me many teaching tools that she had gathered throughout her own children's public-school years.

Turning one of my bedrooms into a preschool room, I added books, blocks and bells to the class room. My walls were decorated with colorful posters of the alphabets, numbers, shapes, and all kinds of animals. My girlfriend gave me many, many work books and worksheets to teach my new preschoolers. These were things that she had gathered throughout the years, from her own children attending the local elementary. With this information, I was actually homeschooling my sons already. My reputation was helped along by my girlfriend's recommendations.

She referred everyone that she couldn't take to me, it was great.

So, another year passed by and it was time for my son to start kindergarten. Following my girlfriend's example again, I pinned the bus shaped pass on my son's shirt and walked him to the bus stop. Feeling some relief, because her children were on the same bus. I was so glad that they were very good friends. I exhaled somewhat, but my heart was still aching. I couldn't shake that feeling, something was incomplete.

I remembered hearing the conversations of the mothers surrounding me, and on how happy they were. I can see that homeschooling mother at the park with her children, she looked happy, but a peaceful happiness. These bus mothers just looked relieved and hurried. I didn't like that at all. I wanted what that lone mother on the park bench had.

Then, throughout the kindergarten year, the reports started to come home in his book bag. "He is showing aggressive behavior," "He is having trouble focusing," "He can't sit still." This was a five-year-old, healthy, well balanced, physically maturing boy. He was a normal boy, in-spite of my short comings of being a single mom at the time. Oh, how I was being pulled to a new dimension. My mind was starting to blossom.

Empowerment

As another year went by, I continued to run the daycare from my apartment. My son was finishing up kindergarten, and my fiancé was talking about marrying me. He intended to move us into a new home in another school district. Yet, I was still just going through the predetermined motions of school life for my son. I started to monitor his behavior by volunteering in his class. I was doing public school because I had not yet gained the courage to start homeschooling.

Then it happened, the very thing that the mystery woman warned me about. The teachers from the elementary school put together a letter that stated I needed to take my son to what they called "Child Find." This was a mental health program, a state-run team of psychotherapist, special educators, and speech language pathologists. They evaluate children that are determined to exhibit traits of ADHD, behavioral problems, and learning disabilities. These children were identified and labeled as uncontrollable or delayed, by the classroom teacher or some other school authority.

The school was insisting that I take him to be evaluated. Therefore, since I didn't know my rights and because I was listening to other mothers from my neighborhood, I was scared. Some of these mothers had been given the same instructions at one point in their lives. I panicked and believed that if I did not get the evaluation, I could be charged with child abuse. Oh no, What! I couldn't believe it. So, needless to say we went to the evaluation. I was so intimidated. I certainly did not want to lose my children. It turned out that the evaluation proved to confirm my beliefs about my son's mental health and academic abilities. I knew what I had taught him before he ever went to school.

Well, there were three young female therapists who worked with my son. It seemed as if they gave him so many tests. With some test he handled objects, while in others he played with toys. They did a hearing test, an eye test and had him write things. I do not know exactly what they were looking for, but I found out when it was over. The young ladies concluded that my son was more than likely bored in his class. That he was well advanced and probably not given enough challenging work. Yes, I knew it! I knew that my boy was intelligent and healthy. You won't believe what they suggested. These ladies told me, that my son would probably be more challenged being HOMESCHOOLED!!!

Yes, they did! I was surprised and pleased. I took my copy of that final report and tucked it securely away along with all my other important documents. This was so awesome, elating, vindicating, and confirming.

How many times did I need to be hit with a confirmation before I recognized the hand of God? This was 'beast', the very thing that I needed to move forward. On the other hand, we still didn't know anyone else that was homeschooling. None of my close friends, no one in my family, and it was still an intimidating choice I needed to make. I hadn't met anyone who homeschooled at the churches we visited. It was still just a concept and dream locked inside my heart. I didn't have the courage to do it. I couldn't find the key of faith to help me step out. Shortly after that meeting, the man that I was dating asked me to marry him. I accepted, and he moved us into a new home, new neighborhood, and new school district. We found a new church family and began to settle in. This was our home church. We were so blessed because we came to learn that there were many homeschooling families in the church, and that the Pastor, himself, homeschooled.

Things were looking positive, and our neighborhood was brand new and more diverse. I learned from the neighbors that the schools were pretty descent. The elementary school that my son would attend was a newly built school.

My son was now going into the first grade, and I thought, OK, maybe this would be a better environment for him. Meanwhile, I was starting to grow in the word of God and beginning to recognize His voice a little more clearly.

Some of the women from our new church began sharing their homeschool stories with me. They gave me books and informative literature about homeschooling. Some of the families were finishing up with their journeys.

Their children were graduating and going to college. This church even had a homeschool band and a coop that met on a weekly basis.

One of the most wonderful things about my new church was that many of the homeschooling families were black. This was the first time I had met black homeschoolers. I could see that they were educated and confident people. Everyone reached out to us, giving me advice and inviting me to their homes. Although the picture was becoming clearer within my mind, I still had not found the courage to transition into homeschooling.

As the year went by my children were participating in various activities within the church. As my husband and I became very involved, my desire to homeschool was once again lulled to sleep. Although it remained deep down inside my heart, churning for release. Yet, I let it lay. Everything seemed to be going well with my son, as he advanced through the first grade, at the new school. Then I started noticing him being a little frazzled when he got home in the evenings. I didn't know what the cause was, but he definitely seemed to be just tired and frustrated all of the time.

One day as we sat down stairs in the basement of our new home, he had just recently gotten home from school. Something about his demeanor was off, as if he carried a heavy burden. I asked him to go upstairs to put something into the trash can that sat on the back deck of our home. I heard him walk up the stairs and out the back door.

My heart just filled with sadness for him, because I knew he had locked himself out. I also knew that he would be frustrated.

Just as I suspected, he came walking down the back deck stairs, sobbing. I opened the sliding door for him and he fell into my arms, weeping profusely. I thought, what on earth could be causing this? He has locked himself out before, and with a big grin on his face, would knock for me to let him back in. He wasn't a solemn kind of child. This cry was filled with some deep hurt, and I had no idea where it was coming from.

Once he was able to calm his heart, I was then able to talk with him about his day. Only to find out that his teacher was very mean.

He said that she would yell at them for doing something wrong. He was terrified of her. Wow, oh my gosh, I didn't know! Because he had never said anything about it. This boy had been enduring verbal abuse from his teacher on a daily basis. He was afraid to do anything wrong. That's why a small thing like locking himself out of the house had him so outdone. He felt like a failure at something that was so simple.

The next day, when I walked him to the bus stop, I talked with the parents of some of the children that were in the same class as my son.

I found out that nearly every one of those children at that bus stop felt the same way. One mother said that her daughter would literally become physically sick in the mornings, when she just thought about going to school. She told me that she had already complained about this teacher's affect upon her daughter to the school principal.

This was the final kick in my backside. I was floored. Angry at myself for allowing my son to be bullied by some overgrown, punk of a woman. Everything within me wants to say her name as I am writing this down, but I won't, for it is over.

I remembered who my Father was. I remembered that my children and I deserved better. I refused to do this anymore.

Working with What I Had

After registering my official complaints to the school about this teacher, I initiated my plan to pull my son out and my second son and any future sons. I had had enough. My children would never, ever be subjected to that kind of tyranny again. Well, this decision was profound for us, because we ended up having two more sons. That is four boys that we will have to safely raise to manhood. I didn't have any more patience with the school system, my faith in it had run out. Not long before I received this insight I watched a documentary, on PBS. It was about a study conducted by a woman whose name is Jane Elliot. The title was "Blue eyes, Brown eyes." This study, in an extremely visual way showed how negative comments, preconceived ideas, and constant ridicule can change a person's mental state. The teacher in the documentary separated and reacted negatively toward every child with brown eyes. The experiment was very successful in proving the teachers point. She demonstrated how a person, especially a young child would be made to feel inferior under such circumstances. This experiment served to open my eyes even more. Was the my child of color targeted? Is he most likely to be accused of having extreme behavior? I cringed at the thought of this happening to my sons. Looking back, I now can understand why I had been given the command to home school.

Throughout the entire experience with my son, I shared my thoughts, hopes and dreams with my husband. He listened, asked questions about what I wanted to do, and how I wanted to do it. This was a new line of thinking for both of us, because we didn't know a thing about homeschooling. But, my man knew me. He understood that I would give my whole self to this task. Not just some halfhearted attempt. So, with his blessing, I examined all the information that I had collected over the years. I met with many of the homeschooling moms from my church, to pick their minds about where I should start. I'll tell you, early on, God literally walked me through the maze of it all. I would find out that He had already placed mentors in my path. Women who had already gone through the complete process. Women who were midway and some who were just starting off. My pastor's wife homeschooled, and she seemed to be very happy doing so. She and the pastor encouraged Michael and I strongly through this adventure. It was such a blessing to have a pastor that supported our choice to homeschool.

Since I had a second grader and a kindergartener, I started out teaching from the 'unschooled' perspective. I didn't settle upon a particular curriculum, or class room setting at first. I was able to successfully do it this way because, in the earlier stages of finding which path to take, I had an experienced mama mentor. She showed me step by step how to put a simple study together. I really wanted to use this approach to teach every subject. I was so excited for my children to learn about numbers, letters, insects, people, and God. My goal was to allow them to choose what interested them. Then I was going to use this method to present it to them, from a biblical perspective, everything that they wanted to learn.

My worldview had been changing all this time. Even before I discovered that having an unfocused, unconscious worldview is really to have a devilish point of view. I had learned from the pastor of my new church that the Word of God says, "To not surrender to God in total submission is to be Godless, even if it's done in ignorance." "My people suffered because of lack of knowledge" – Hosea4:6. Once, I accepted the Judeo-Christian Faith, I had to understand and accept this reality. Realizing that there was no middle ground when it came to Christianity, I either was for God or I was not. In my own life, that is what I had, devilish thoughts. It is why I lived the way that I lived.

All my previous decisions where never thoroughly thought out. My thoughts were most often surface thinking. Up to this point I was truly a dead man walking. It was as if my mind was turned off to the power of Gods Holy Spirit.

Ephesians 2:1-5

"And you *He made alive,* who were dead in trespasses and sins, ²in which you once walked according to the course of this world, according to the prince of the power of the air, the spirit who now works in the sons of disobedience, ³ among whom also we all once conducted ourselves in the lusts of our flesh, fulfilling the desires of the flesh and of the mind, and were by nature children of wrath, just as the others.

⁴ But God, who is rich in mercy, because of His great love with which He loved us, ⁵ even when we were dead in trespasses, made us alive together with Christ (by grace you have been saved),"

Now I understood why it took me so long to finally act upon the plans that He was weaving right before my eyes.

It is the reason why I never considered I could teach my own children. I didn't know his thoughts. I can't express myself enough how very important this process was for me, and I suspect it will be for many of you. We must make our decisions, with deeply pondered thought. Especially when it comes to homeschooling. This is a choice that 'you' are making for them. You must be sensitive to the urging of the Holy Spirit. You have to almost try and think like God. Being able to see their future. Your children's educational future will be in your hands. As the parent, it will be your responsibility to make sure that they are given all that they will need to succeed. Now, hold on, don't feel discouraged, you can do it. I know that you can, because you love your child with all your heart. Your child was given to you from God. No other being can create a brand-new human life, place that life inside the body of another human being, naturally. To homeschool is a major decision for you to make as a parent. My decision to homeschool was nourished, by many years of discovery. I had to find out who I was first, and then I learned 'whose' I was.

During the two years that my son was in the public school system, I was learning how to be a protective mother, a true wife, a purposeful learner and a spiritually led soul.

Implementing in the Lives of My Sons What I Learned from God's Word.

Since, I didn't have the educational background of a school teacher I needed to learn rapidly. I needed someone who could help me develop parenting skills. I accepted that I would need to call upon the experiences of others to guide some of my choices.

First, I decided to follow the parenting examples that I read about in God's Word. I thought, OK, I need to train these kids in the way that they should go according to the word of God, Prov22:6. Hmm, so just how am I supposed to do that? So, I searched God's word, reading stories about some of the mothers in the Bible, and observing God's actions as He prepared someone to serve Him.

The following pattern began to form in my mind as I read these stories:

1. I saw that God was always there.

2. That his commitment to his children stood concretely, no matter where they went.

3. That He administered swift and sure discipline when sinned against.

4. I noticed that God taught His own how to live in the world where they existed.

5. He taught them how to be themselves. Standing against the strong forces of the opposition to their very existence.

6. God instilled steel like character within their very bones.

7. I saw that God flooded His children with His foundational truth. Afterwards, He put them to the test by placing them in the hands of those who opposed Him.

This last point, really stuck in my head, because I had done the opposite. I placed my tenderhearted son in someone else hands, before he was able to spell his own name. Oh, man, because of what we experienced with his 1st grade teacher, this point truly hurts my heart.

8. Something else I noticed from the Word, God always seemed to allow some measure of suffering. Then, He would use that very suffering to craft a servant's heart within His chosen vessel. That chosen one would end up with a developed spirit of humility.

It also seemed that God always provided the best training needed, so that His servant would be equipped to walk in his gift.

If that servant needed to learn how to lead, He gave him plenty sheep to shepherd as in the case of King David. If the servant needed to develop perseverance and hard work, God provided him with manual labor. Moses seemed to have learned this way. Some of His servants trained in the military. Learned archery and how to play musical instruments. God's servants were well rounded individuals, fully equipped to face any situation presented to them. It is extremely curious, how the young David played the harp, using it to calm the spirit of King Saul. Who was a man that was trying to kill him! That was just awesome!

Once we discovered this pattern, we started our track to homeschool the boys. My husband and I put a plan in place that would not only educate their brains but would also train their emotions. We knew that true education needed to teach an individual how to control his human emotions in order to prosper in this world. We were determined to make sure that these boys understood that we expected their complete loyalty. They would have our total commitment to their growth, as they were being groomed into men. We established the rule that we would be their mentors. Under no circumstances would they turn to any other person outside our family for leadership. Now, this may seem harsh at first glance, but not when I consider the state that young people are in today, especially the male child. Young boys need to know how to become strong, dedicated leaders of their own existence. Think about the amount of time people dedicate in training their animals. Shouldn't our children receive just as much of our attention.

In a lot of countries, we train our dogs so that they will give us absolute loyalty. Giving extreme attention to the ones that will earn us the show ribbon. We put in countless hours training our horses, so that they will become world class performers. We place so much effort in developing things, because we want certain results. Well, our boys meant more to us than any dog or horse. So, if ever anyone challenged our methods, I just asked of them one curious question "Do you have any pets?"

Therefore, within God's guidelines, we intentionally set a course that would guide them towards excelling wherever they chose to go. Since, we wanted to influence their growth toward God. We set strict rules during the early stages of their growth, in hopes of developing men who would be strong leaders. We realized that if our boys were in the public school, that they would be encouraged to go to the school counselor or the teacher for life advice. We knew that in some schools, children are encouraged to seek out advice from all other adults before going to their own parents. I think not! We never allowed anyone to step in for us when our boys needed to be re-directed.

As their mom, if I told my boys to do something and they acted as if they weren't hearing me, I implemented strong repercussions. I don't mean that I had to spank them for every little misbehavior. Yet, they were never confused about what we expected when it came to their loyalty to our parental leadership. Training your kids in this matter will get you some ugly criticism from some people.

Yet, we were able to cultivate character and a sense of self-respect within our sons. Today we are always complimented for the way our sons have matured into well rounded young men. This character building was our goal from the start.

Continuing to follow the pattern that we found in God's Word, we gave our total commitment to the training of our sons. My husband was hardworking, committed, and an extremely loyal father. He gave any and everything needed for these boys to be successful. Since, I would be the main one teaching on the academic side, I begin to compile a list of items that I wanted to use during the school year. Further researching and being certain about what the boys needed for each grade level. Ensuring that the books I chose met the requirements of the Virginia Standards of Learning.

After sharing my choices with my husband, and because he trusted my book choices, I got the go ahead to purchase.

I would like to point out something here. Even though the boys were young, I realized that they were super in tuned to us. They were always listening to our interaction. As I went over the curriculum choices with Dad, explaining to him how these books would fit in our homeschool, the kids were often right there. The boys heard daddy asking me questions, then affirming my choices. This simple interaction modeled commitment, as well as, demonstrating the loyalty we had for one another. Remember learning is not only gleaned from text books, children practice what we preach in all aspects of our modeling behaviors.

I was also painfully aware that because I was divorced and remarried, some people questioned my commitment. Once I overheard a woman make a sarcastic remark about divorced women. She said it as we sat at a table together during a women's luncheon. This woman knew full well that I was divorced and remarried. Yet, she let the words cross her lips anyway. I thought to myself, I will have to prove that I am capable of being committed to my children and my husband. Because my husband was not the biological father of my two older sons, his character was being observed. Since I didn't have a college degree I felt that my educational limitations were being scrutinized. We picked up on these indirect little shades during this time. Although, we felt that some people were looking at us from the outside and watching for inconsistencies. Our boys were developing concrete ideas about life and about us. So, we tried to model commitment and loyalty, imperfect as we were.

1 Corinthians 1:27 (NIV)

But God chose the foolish things of the world to shame the wise; God chose the weak things of the world to shame the strong.

I could see that His will was for us to be committed to the growth of our children, and I trusted that He would bless our honest efforts.

Teach Them Your Actual Name or They Will Call You Mommy

One thing I learned earlier on was that, even though my children were young they needed to know the truth. I believed that I needed to teach them about the world that they lived in and I needed to use correct wording. I began to understand this fact during the years of doing daycare for other people's children.

What I mean is that a lot of these children had some wacky ideas about life and how it functioned. One example was how babies came into the world. Once I overheard my sons and two brothers that I did day care for, talking about this very thing. "My mommy said that God put babies on a big slide that comes from heaven. That's where babies come from" the older of the brothers shouted. My son, "No they don't. My mommy said that God lets the mommy and the daddy make the baby!" The two younger siblings were just listening. They debated back and forth for a while until coming to a dead end. Then I heard multiple footsteps running towards me. Needless to say, we had to have a conversation about where babies came from, on their level of course.

Another time when my son was in school, kindergarten, I realized that he didn't know my real name. Whenever someone asked him, what is your mother's name? He would answer "mommy." These two incidents helped to mold my thinking about using real talk with my sons.

We don't want our children going around thinking silly things, unnecessarily. I believe that this type of life training academically handicaps our children, before they even get a chance to start the race.

So, with that conviction, I made sure that I used the accurate words to explain and describe things for my boys. If I needed to explain something about their bodies, I used correct words. Like penis, vagina, nipples, sex (the word), snout, vomit, white, black, (persons). Any word that some would cringe at when talking to a child. Whether you know it or not, children are very perceptive and have probably heard some of these things already. You need to be the one that teaches them about these kinds of things, or someone else will. Only when they do, most of the time the instructions will be exaggerated, conflicting or just wrong. Of course, this is exactly where Satan wants your child. So, understand we don't have to sugar coat everything for our children. They are very intelligent human beings, but just a little smaller then we are. Because, God has also endowed them with His image we have to be precise. So, it is our job as parents to make sure that the children God has given to us comprehend the growth that He will surely take them through.

Utilizing the Henry Ford Tactic "Finding a Man or Woman in Five Minutes"

Now I was at the point where I wanted to expand upon all the wonderful things that my kids and I had dreamt up. As time passed, I had collected many different curriculum ideas. I now felt the need to pick one so that we could keep moving. Trouble is I didn't know if I was starting right or even if I had the best books. I needed to once again consult the wisdom of a veteran who had already gone through the homeschool steps. Someone who understood the level where I was at the time. I had a second grader and a kindergartener, and I wanted to correlate their work.

I remember something that I had read about Henry Ford, the famous automobile mogul. A quote that is attributed to him anyway, "I can find a man or woman in five minutes that knows what I don't."

Let me tell you, this quote was like an affirmation that kept me walking forward in the decision to homeschool my children. I know that God had allowed me to read this quote and to keep it in my mind to build confidence within me. Every time I thought that I did not know something, or heard or seen a thing before, I'd remember that quote. You guys believe me when I tell you that the energy from this quote that was buried deeply within my psyche became a living thing. It took on legs and arms and moved me to where I needed to look.

Through this affirmation, God guided my thinking to the exact person that would help me to solve the problem. Sometimes, this would be complete strangers. I don't mean something weird happening. Yet, the help would come from a librarian, or a person whom I really didn't know too well from the church. Other times help would come from someone that happened to be sitting next to me on the bench at one of my son's various sports activities. There was always someone that I could turn to.

Remember, this is how I got started with homeschooling in the first place. He sent a complete stranger to me. This stranger commanded me to homeschool the two small boys whom I was holding hands with, as we were walking into Safeway store! My God has never ever left me in want during this journey. I just knew and I trusted that He would provide what we needed. He always did.

I hope that I am not making you angry or bored by talking about God and energy or strangers. I am writing this to you many years after going through it. As I recall the journey, it just causes my heart to pound with joy. Especially when I think about how God's guiding hands brought us through. It was not a fake halfhearted attempt either, it was absolute divine direction.

There were times when I didn't quite get it. But somehow the direction would become clear, and I would look back from the other end. Thinking, wait a minute, I figured this out. We accomplished a thing. Then, within my soul I felt Him light up my insides with His presence. Whispering, "Yes, Adrienne you finally opened your mind to me". So, it isn't that I am always this obedient person kingly attuned to God's voice.

No, this journey was and still is a walk of sanctifying education for my entire family, especially for me.

Equipped with this guiding mantra, I set out to find my way through the homeschooling maze. It was indeed a maze for me, because I had just embarked upon it. Looking at all the information that I had received from different people, and trying to discern which was best for me, I had to make a choice. But, what ever shall I do?

"Friends that are College Graduates and Fellow Homeschoolers"

As I worked through this change in how we did school, I was talking with many of the families who were already long into educating their own children. These talks and visit were my teachers training. I picked up some wonderful insights. Like how many of the fathers where very active in their children's educational development. These men held strong convictions about their children's development. In many families, the mother did most of the instructing during the day. The father did what was needed when he came home in the evening. I found it so fascinating how these families approached it. Neither was a carbon copy of the other, each seemed to be unique but effective in their methods. All the families were open and friendly towards me, showing genuine eagerness to help me get along with my journey.

It reminded me of the family that I met in the very beginning of my divinely lead journey. It was so awesome to discover that there were so many choices and so many successful examples for me to glean from.

So, in the beginning of our homeschooling days I would gather my two little boys and make my way to someone's house for a "play date". Of course, I was going to learn just how to do this homeschool thing. I needed to see it in actions. This is one of the better and fastest ways to build your own confidence when you are just starting out. Please search out these opportunities, go with a childlike faith until you can walk on your own.

One of the very first ladies that helped me was Sherry Petritone. She lived in a gated community, in a huge house that I couldn't even imagine affording at the time. When I drove up into the driveway, I started to get this sinking feeling that I was way out of my class. I can't do this. I can't afford this.

It's amazing how the devil tries to convince you that God is a liar and isn't there to help you through things. The whole beautiful scene of her home before my eyes began to drive me down up under a thick cloud of defeat. I was scared.

As I began to panic within my heart I almost couldn't hear the mantra playing in the background of my mind over my increasing heartbeat.

"I can find a man in five minutes, I can find a man in five minutes" my mind kept playing that mantra over and over. Using this phrase as the catapult, God pushed me out of that car. He helped me to gather my boys and He moved me up the walkway. Still feeling a little unworthy, I walked forward with a nervous smile on my face. As I got closer, she opened the door, with such a huge smile on her face that it instantly relaxed me. Her children stood there smiling and welcoming my little boys into their home. I thought, "Maybe it's going to be alright after all."

While the children played, she showed me all around her home. I saw that every room had some evidence of educational paraphernalia. It was unlike a quiet stern library, books were stacked in almost every room. I loved seeing that, it resonated within my very being for some reasons. She pointed out how they used each of these rooms. Explaining how it really didn't matter about the area you did school in, but that you just needed to equip the room with the right materials.

Like encyclopedias, dictionaries, reference books, and all sorts of National geographic books. You'll need books on animals, books about different countries, books on anything and everything you can think about. She assured me that I didn't need to go broke getting these books either. I learned that they had purchased a lot of these books from library sales, used books stores, and that many came from thrift stores. Wow, it was exciting me to hear this. I began to believe that yes, I can afford this, I can do this. God was helping me to see this pattern. I was so happy and eager.

My friend helped me to understand that teaching my children didn't require expensive books and curriculum. I just had to look in the right places for what my family needed. I was learning just how easy it was to finance my children's education. It became clear that homeschooling was for me and that it was a direct gift from God.

I wondered about how I would test my children's knowledge and academic strength as we homeschooled. Sherry showed me some of the test that she used. I was starting to sweat a little bit because I didn't know how to administer test. How would I know if I'm doing it correctly? How can I tell if they are accurate? This was crazy to even think about. I guess she saw the panic in my face, so she gently put her hand on my shoulder and smiled. "Don't worry it isn't as hard as you think it will be." I felt a little lighter after that affirmation. But, even still my experience with giving any kind of test had been zero.

My friend pointed out that the test was create by Seton Catholic church. Test that I could order and administer myself. I thought, "What! I do not have a college degree". She assured me that I didn't need it, and that I would be able to understand the procedures and administer the test with a little effort. Ok, I was getting excited again. She told me, although she did have a college degree, that the person who helped her get started in homeschooling was a veteran homeschooler.

That person had educated nine children, some who were going into the medical field. She was able to educate her children even though she did not have a college degree herself. Let me encourage you, when you start to fill with self-doubt, and you will. Rest assured your limitations do not have to handicap the children that you want to homeschool. Remember my mantra!

I spent the rest of the morning with this lovely family, soaking in how they did school. The children were bright, well balanced children, genuinely interested in me and my boys. I was pleased with their ability to engage my young sons as if they were parents in training. That's exactly what homeschooling is all about, our children learning, how to do life. They are watching mom model how to care for children, how to manage a home and how to entertain guests. I noticed the boy do things that a father would normally do. Like making sure the door was shut and locked. I saw him check the trash can, and then emptying it. These young children, two girls and a boy were excellent understudies to their parents.

Having a day care in my home for a few years, I could spot a striking difference in their attitudes and their willingness to help the younger children.

I hadn't seen that character in any of the elementary aged children that I cared for in my home. Most of them came with a predetermined belief that they didn't like "little" kids. I had one boy who told me that he didn't like babies. Mind you he said this

while he was looking at my infant. So, to see these young children with the kind of positive attitudes that they had was very refreshing.

That is the beauty of the whole homeschooling model. You get to mold your child in the way that you would like him or her to grow. You can allow your child to flourish into what their destiny is without too much outer influences. You will teach them to be self-motivated. This is seriously important if your goal for them is to be well rounded individuals. Teaching then at home will cause them to imprint upon you and your spouse, not to lock wholeheartedly onto their peers.

So, as the saying goes "The apple doesn't fall to far from the tree", so you had better strive hard to be a good tree!

Engaging My Community

Now that we were into the academics of homeschooling, we added other parts for a complete education. For the first curriculum book set we chose the Horizons series. I liked these books because they had big bright colorful pages. The kids where so excited about their books, as well. I found that these were just what I needed to start off. I was able to purchase a set for each grade level, Kindergarten and 2nd grade. This curriculum was very challenging and came highly recommended from many other homeschoolers, as well as from my girlfriend. Each book covered the entire subject needed for the boys' grade level in language and math. I loved them because I could understand just what to do without needing any extra teachers' curriculum work books.

You see, when you are first starting out, you will be unsure about whether to purchase the teacher guide or not. I can tell you that over the years, I found that I really didn't need them for the elementary grades, particularly not for grades 1 through 4. Most of the teacher guides are designed for a classroom setting. It gives extra advice on how to administer the work and how to pace yourself. This is something that really wasn't an issue in my home with two children. Even if you have more at that grade level, you really can give them their book and let them go at their own pace.

So, as we proceeded, we really engaged this type of learning wholeheartedly. I bought 3 x5 cards and made many sets of my own flash cards. I used these for math as well as language. I would have the boys, mostly my second grader, write down the addition/subtraction facts. I'd challenge them to memorize these cards until the facts became easy. We would put beginner's words on flashcards then draw pictures to help us remember what the word meant. The boys seemed to thrive with this type of learning. I realized that this method helped them to develop in other areas too. Like sketching, hand eye coordination, symmetry and color matching.

For science and history, I would search the library shelves for all kinds of books on different subjects. The boys loved this idea. We would go through the catalog looking for any book that looked interesting. This search was so entertaining, the boys and I would sit in the library for a couple of hours devouring the many gorgeous books on animals and geography. One time my sons were doing this with such quiet enthusiasm, that a lady approached me about becoming a student mentor. She thought that I was a school counselor with these kids under my watch. I'll tell you, getting these books from the library was like finding gold for my boys. I intentionally, chose books with big, gorgeous pictures to hook them. I realized that the boys would spend hours gazing at the pictures and reading the information next to them. I didn't have to force them to read at all. I even sat on the couch right in the middle of them, oohing and aahing over the beautiful pictures. Pictures of beautiful animals, nature scenes or some wonderful shot that totally captivated us. If you are like me, this reading activity will turn into one of your favorite memories with the children.

This early start to learning cultivated a love for reading and learning in my children as well as in me. I took homeschooling very seriously. Not to the point of risking boring my children to death or causing them to hate learning. No, I mean that I did just about everything with them. If they were coloring a page, I printed one for myself and joined them. We made little booklets covering many different subjects. I just embraced it as if I was relearning the thing, which I was. Truly, my mind was beginning to expand and soak in things that I had never learned or had long forgotten. Sometimes It was as if I had not learned a thing at all. I absolutely flourished with my educational growth as I taught my children. My world was flowering all around me. That's how I knew that God was blessing our decision to homeschool the children. He was using that same decision to homeschool me. God was filling in the gaps of my miseducation. He was allowing me to enjoy the things that I had missed when I was being dragged from school district to school district. I was learning the things that I should have learned at that level, instead of having to play the role of mommy for my younger siblings.

Oh yea! I could feel God's presence working in my life with every new discovery. when I saw the sparkle of understanding in the eyes of my children, I thought, hmm, I'm blessed. Thank you, Jesus!

Extra-Curricular Activities

Now that we had settled upon a good academic base, that would carry us through this exciting, yet scary homeschool journey. My husband and I started talking about extra-curricular activities and how to engage our surrounding community even more.

Since the boys were so young, they had not really played any organized sports. Yet, my husband knew that the boys would need some kind of activity. But, what should we start with? Since I would be the one chauffeuring everyone back and forth during the day, I thought I don't want to drive too far away. Well, the years have proven that to be faulty thinking or false hope.

I talked with some of my friends from the homeschool community to find out what sort of activities they participated in. I was pleasantly overwhelmed by the response. These families were doing everything. Unique things, that I knew, if my boys were in public school they wouldn't get a chance to engage in.

They were raising animals for 4h projects, planting gardens, acting in community plays, singing in community choirs, traveling with touring choirs, playing instruments in community bands and home school bands. Some kids were participating in very prestigious band camps. Some of the older kids were leading Sunday school children classes. Other's taught an evening Bible learning class called Awana. Kids were on swim teams, debate teams, playing football, soccer, baseball, rugby, and basketball. One of my favorites was the fencing class. Yes, fencing.

It turned out to be one of the boy's favorite and they were good at it. There were numerous options for us to choose from, for their benefit and for our enjoyment.

Now that the boys were old enough they became interested in football. So, our first team sport was a football team that was led by one of the fathers from our church. We were not looking for this particular benefit, but it was a bonus to have a man from our church being the boy's coach. The boys loved playing football. I on the other hand didn't like seeing all the helmet crushing and knock downs. Yet, over the years I have learned that this was the life of parents with children who loved sports, especially boys. Many of the boy's friends played on this same team. It was a lot of fun, even though I did not know much about football I ran up and down that field cheering them on anyway.

    Well, after football was over, we did the seasonal shuffle just as all the other families were doing. We did baseball, basketball and swimming. We kept these boys so busy, that I knew they wouldn't have time to be bored.

Having the boys participate on the different teams and taking lessons, were some of the ways that we exposed our children to the leadership of other adults. We felt that it was important for our children to learn how to follow instructions from someone else other than us. Yet, we chose who that instructor would be, by choosing the team or class our sons would participate in. This part is important, because of two reasons, one was, I did notice that some of the children had a problem with taking instruction from anyone other than their own parents. I don't know if they were naturally rebellious or they just didn't trust the instructor. Whichever it was, I recognized that that could become a potential problem for my kids. Especially if they had this attitude while pursuing higher education or even in a work environment with a future boss. Outside activities will help with this. So please do not shelter your kids so much that they see everyone else as weird or evil. You may think that I am exaggerating, but I taught Sunday school with a lot of homeschooled kids, and some acted exactly like this with me. It was rather sad.

Once we got the sports routine picked out and established, it was time for other kinds of activities. Now I needed to add classes that would enrich the boy's lives in different areas.

They were older now and I wanted them to learn an instrument. This was something that I had never gotten the opportunity to do as a child, and I wanted them to at least have the exposure to playing music. So once again, I set up visit dates with my experienced homeschooling friends. Nearly all these friends played instruments. I had no experience with playing at all, and I couldn't even read music at the time. So, I soaked in all their knowledge, gladly accepting their offers to teach my boys. That is one characteristic that I found over and over. Many families were very eager to help others learn. It was so neat to find this kind of atmosphere. Once again, my God sent people into my life that taught me in so many ways. People that looked just like me, that were intelligent and financially secure. They were at ease in their own skin. This doesn't seem like a bonus for those who have never had to conjure up this kind of strength. Yet, God understands.

My sons' first instrument teacher was an ex-military sweetheart that absolutely loved music and loved seeing children flourish. She had six children of her own, who all owned and played an instrument. Boy, I was at a loss at first. My boys weren't even renting instruments at that time. So, Mary Wofford was so gracious, and so determined to teach my boys, that she allowed them to use her horns until we got our own. This was truly a blessing because it helped us to experience the sound and feel of many different horns before we needed to purchase one.

I listened to Mary's children play trumpets, tubas (which Mary played herself), saxophones, French horns and I think there was a trombone. At the time, I didn't know the difference and certainly couldn't distinguish between the sounds of each instrument. But over the years, I would learn to recognize each instruments sound and grow to love band.

Although this opportunity was embarked upon for my kids, it really did enrich my soul and sharpened my ear for music. As the children were growing in their abilities to play the instruments, I was learning how to read music and Mary taught me how to help them at home. I think that this became as second nature to me, I loved music. Especially, rich tones that paired the melodic sound of the horns and woodwinds together like a symphonic love affair. Whoa! Wait a minute, where did that poetic sentence come from? You see that's what I mean, once I started helping my children to learn their instruments, I was being awakened too. My heart and mind started to understand how music had the ability to reach out to your soul.

I was beginning to understand patterns and relationships between music and other parts of life.

This revelation excited me so much that I wanted to sing, to play an instrument, and wanted to learn something new. My very thoughts caused my husband to bring home an organ, I really do believe that. It seemed as though when I desired something, God heard my cry while it was still within my mind. Because, many times I thought of a thing and my husband would walk through the door with that very specific thing. I am not exaggerating, it would be given to me as I desired. The thing was not always brand new from a store, but I would receive what I desired to have. I know that it was so that my intellect would grow, so that my faith would be sealed, and so that I would progress through 'my" homeschooling adventure. This grand organ proved to be another one of those best gifts from God.

I began using this organ to help me find sounds that matched the instruments as the kids practiced. We would sing together, working out the melodies and harmony of many different songs. We learned to understand so much about music using that old organ and I treasured the times that we spent together as a family. My husband was even able to sit at the organ to work out the notes to a song that he and his men's vocal group ended up performing. Don't forget that my husband had no prior music training, but yet he wrote the music and words for that song. See, I told you God was working it out in our lives.

Well, we finally did purchase instruments for our children, a place that allowed us to rent to own or pay out right for them. We started out with the rent to own plan and then paid them off with our tax refund money. It worked out just fine that way.

The kids were getting better at playing. So they were actually invited to play with the homeschool band that Mary was conducting. They played for her church congregation and other venues. It was a very nice opportunity for the boys to get that band exposure. I am telling you this to help you to see how easy and freeing it was to integrate such enrichment into the lives of my children while I homeschooled them. You can find such impactful choices for your family as well.

My children's interest in playing instruments caught the eye of another homeschooling family in our own home church. When they were recognized it opened them up to start playing in our own church. The Mom and Dad were musicians and they had three young musicians who were well trained. Their mom was a pianist, and she also loved to teach. The relationship with Percy & Cynthia Robinson opened us up to so many different avenues to perform and receive expert instructions. She introduced me to many band instructors who were veteran teachers in the public school and some conducted community orchestras. My son who played the saxophone auditioned and got in the youth community orchestra of one of these instructors.

Many years went by as we homeschooled, but the thing that we cultivated the most was music and the playing of instruments. All the boys ended up playing in many different bands, orchestras and singing with choirs that traveled. This time in their lives was such an enriching atmosphere. Any family that is contemplating homeschooling, but is worried about socialization, put it to rest. Your children will be socialized, only it will be in a more controlled and parent directed atmosphere. Even when our son played with the youth orchestra, we were somewhere around to monitor him. One of us dropped him off and picked him up, he was never left alone to just roam the halls of the high school where they practiced.

When it came to my children learning other skills that 'I' didn't have, I diligently searched for outside help. One particular year when I now had all four boys, we joined a co-op. This was so that they could participate in elective type classes, like Biology, Writing, History, Music and Art. These classes were very exciting, and we were deeply involved. They were administered by the moms of most of the children there. Many of whom had advance degrees and loved the subject that they taught. I chose this type of atmosphere to get my children exposed to a classroom setting, yet still be parent controlled. Believe me when I say that it was not some simple-minded teaching. The women knew their subjects. I thought the children gained so much out of the classes. One month, they constructed our entire solar system with foam balls. I remember helping in this class. It was awesome to watch the children's eyes light up when they held the sun, planets and moon in their hands. I loved painting replicas of the solar system, copying from the posters hanging around the class room. Each child constructed their own solar system to hold and take home. My boys got home and placed them on the ceiling of their rooms right away. I still have some of those foam ball planets hanging around here.

Another class that I thoroughly enjoyed was the Art class, in which the boys wrote the words and drew the pictures for their own books. Some of the older kids embellished their pages with gorgeous photos and beautifully fonted manuscripts. I mean, my good friend, Dena Jacques, who organized the entire co-op, really put them to work to make these books. She actually read each book, wrote reviews, solicited reviews from others, took press pictures and made a huge deal out of it. One of my boys wrote a comic book which he illustrated. Another one of my sons did a nature book using pictures from the national geographic magazine. I really enjoyed helping them with the process of putting these books together. Because of this class, my sons really learned to love making up characters and stories. This cultivated a love for the written word within their spirits. I learned that this last benefit of something sealing within their spirit was so important for gaining in all other subject as well. When your child is excited about a thing, and is really enjoying doing it, he or she will soar. So, as the teaching parent, watch for these jewels in educating your child, so that you can use them to your fullest advantage!

Testing

One other extreme benefit that I received from participating in this co-op was the access to testing!!!! Yes, not only were the academics on a superb level, the children were able to sit in a classroom. Well not a traditional class room, but a similar setting. It was fun to have them being able to test in a group setting occasionally. I didn't really realize it at the time, but this practice laid the foundation for them when the time came to take the officially administered SAT, and ACT tests.

Although there are families that do not use testing of any kind, I believe testing can be very helpful in assessing your child's progress. When you provide this type of atmosphere for your child to actively experience the testing process, it will give you a better understanding, as to how your child will react. When the child is in the room where the test will count for him or count against him, this is not the time to learn that he has panicked.

Although, I did stop the primary school testing, once they were old enough to take the college entrance test. But, still I appreciated knowing whether or not my boys were able to function and understand procedures in a traditional testing environment.

Sometimes, we think that this is a natural ability for them to have but let me assure you it is not. Testing is a foreign skill that must be practiced, just like memorizing the multiplication facts. I watched each of my sons walk through the testing process and found out that each one had a different reaction to testing.

My baby son in particular, had it a little harder when it came to practicing testing. Since our environment had changed somewhat when it was time for him to learn how to test. We no longer had the benefit of a coop at our disposal, and it showed up big time. When it was time for him to take the ACT and SAT, he froze. He had a fear of testing due to unfamiliarity of the procedures, so he messed up. He tested well at home with the end of unit test and all. But, when it came to taking the test that counted and really mattered his brain just froze. Although he knew how to transfer his answers from his book to the answer sheet, he felt so pressured from the fact that the test was timed that he forgot to do so. It required him retaking the test many times before he felt relaxed enough to complete the test correctly. We had to do this to get his score to where it needed to be for college entrance. Because my other three sons were relaxed and successful at taking these exams, I didn't learn this lesson about fear until the last son was in the testing room. So, I would advise everyone to find a resource that will expose the child to the process of test taking. Even if you don't think that this method is for you, you must think about what is best for your child.

Over the years, we have learned that there is no one way, cookie cut method to educating a young one. Each child is an individual and each child's education must be tailored to him or her. Besides, that is the beauty of homeschooling and this is something that you can absolutely accomplish through your homeschool adventure.

Now, here are the names of some of the places that provides nationally accepted test. Seton Testing Services offers the CAT (California Achievement Test) test for each grade level. This is a test that any parent can administer on his or her own. It is a test that is accepted in every state and evaluates every needed academic area, to include writing. I do recommend the writing part, because writing is required for entrance at many colleges. Once we completed the CAT test, I just mailed it to Seton and they would grade it. I loved doing these tests when my children were younger. It was so revealing and rewarding to see their progress. I could see where they had holes in their understanding and I would adjust their studies accordingly. One other Test that Seton offered is the Iowa Test. This test must be administered by someone with a bachelor's degree. I welcomed this procedure, because it gave my children the opportunity once again to be tested by someone other than me. The results were strictly in someone else's hands. It also helped to boost my confidence in what I had taught during the teaching period.

I am sure that there are many other tests or methods to assess your child's comprehension and progress. These are some of the tools that we utilized when the time came for our sons to be evaluated. When my children became eligible to take the SAT and ACT, I stopped the primary testing and focused on these two. Our goal was college, so these are the tests that we used to demonstrate that our sons were fully ready for college.

We solicited the services of a specialist Dr. Rowe, to work with our sons, and he took them through rigorous practice until the time of testing. Some of my boys took the test more than once, always reaching for a better score. Depending on which college the son wanted to attend, this dictated what score was needed. So, this is where we invested money to get them what was required. Do I dare say that it has "paid off?" Two of my sons are college graduates, the third is about to start his junior year and my baby is a college freshman. I know that college is not the only way for one to find purpose. But it was a real goal for us.

Intentional Training

I heard someone say or maybe I read it somewhere that "It takes intentional action on the part of someone else to properly groom children for a successful future."

I agree with this one hundred percent. Moving from the divine to the world here are some examples: John the Baptist, The Prophet Samuel, Israel's King David, The Kennedy's, The Jackson's, Michael Jordan, Tiger woods, Serena and Venus Williams, Ben Carson,

Simone Biles. I'm sure there are many more that I haven't listed, but they are awesome examples of this quote.

My husband and I knew from the beginning that we would have to approach parenting our children in a completely radical way, totally different from the way we were parented. My husband came from a more traditional home. With a dad and mom both present all the time, he was properly parented. His dad didn't take him by the hand to show him how to be a dad, his dad walked it for him.

Michael's father was a man who was so focused on keeping his family together, focused on providing them a place to live, and giving them food to eat, that when he got home he was worn out and spent. But I can see that my husband's father taught him how to love in action, how to persevere, and how to be responsible for his own family. My husband speaks of his father in such a loving nurturing way, that there is no mistaking that his father left a foundational mark upon his soul. Sometimes, I think that these things are better parental patterns rather than someone just mouthing the words 'I love you.'

Now, when you consider my upbringing, well, let's just say it's a wonder I am sitting here writing this book for you. I didn't have a father in the home, my world was abruptly redirected when my siblings, and I were taken from our mother and were split up. We were corralled into three different family members' homes where I suffered an even worse abusive environment.

I didn't have one example of a normal home with traditional parents caring for their children. In my immediate family I was surrounded by strong willed women who took on the role of both mom and dad, but many times the children where splintered. Almost all of them became lost in a world of sin and self-destruction. As I was slipping toward the darkest path, it is only by the grace of God that I was able to claw my way out.

It is funny how my life has turned out as far as parenting is concerned. I too ended up in a divorced situation, instantly becoming a single mom. I was determined not to allow my sons to be splintered into another statistical story line.

My parenting role was given another chance when I remarried. My husband helped me to be the mother and wife that I always knew that I could be.

I believed that God, the grand weaver could take old good for nothing lives and turn them out to be used for His glory and for their own good.

Therefore, I believe that I cultivated the mindset that I had about parenting. 'Intentional' is the operative word for my actions. Particularly my actions in the parenting part, remember I was the one home with the children daily. I was responsible for purchasing the curriculum, locating the classes, finding the coaches, enrolling the boys in lessons, driving them to and fro. So, I had to concoct a battle plan for getting all these things done. It didn't matter about my stormy past flaws. My children couldn't wait for me to 'find' myself. They couldn't wait for me to get partying out of my system. I understood that I had to be a parent right now, in "their" present.

This wasn't easy either, for I didn't have modeled examples to pull from my past experiences. So, armed with the best model there is in the world, my Bible, and the new examples from the married couples in my church, I pushed on with my charge. I knew from reading how God equipped His children that I had to continually knock on doors, searching for the right opportunities for my sons. So, when He showed me an opportunity, I pursued it relentlessly.

Observance taught me that people who went towards something halfheartedly rarely reached their goals, but those that pushed forward until they had exhausted the line, usually did reach their goals. This is a lesson that God showed me, and one I often tried to teach my children. Anything worth having is going to cost you something. You can't expect to receive positive results without some kind of sacrifice.

You must be willing and ok with setting your personal ambitions aside, until you have accomplished what is best for your children's education and lives.

With this mindset, we understood that the first step in homeschooling and raising children would mean that you had to give up self. Your goals had to take the second seat to your children's future. We adopted this belief because ultimately it was our decision to homeschool the children. At the inception of the decision, they had no choice in the matter. So, we had to be willing to give them our all.

My husband always says, "Homeschooling isn't for everyone." Not that everyone can't do it. He says this because you must be dedicated to producing the best results as you possibly can for the child's sake. You as the parent must figure out how to manage your life, the children's lives and still be able to provide the needed relationship for your marriage. This way of living and raising a family is not to be taken lightly; it does require tremendous sacrifice on the part of the parents. Specifically, the mother, when the father is the primary bread winner.

So, for me, I had to rely heavily upon the new concepts of marriage that were around me and what I was learning from the word of God. Oh, I was not a seasoned Christian, I wasn't a saint, neither was I even close to being a Bible scholar. But I just naively trusted that if I opened my heart to the prompting of Gods voice that He would lead me where I needed to go.

Once I perceived what tendencies my sons were moving towards, I intentionally guided them in that direction. Sure, I knew that they all needed to have the basic academics down, such as counting, math, reading, spelling, history, science, etc. So, I made sure that we focused on getting a solid grasp on these things first of all.

I would make them write out the times tables on flash cards. I made them drill each other or I would drill them all together with the facts. This always created a desire within them to do their best because of a little thing called competition. It was a fun time.

I would help them to see the relationship of math in our everyday life. We counted stairs, cars, apples, signs, anything that had a rhyme or reason, we used them in the learning process. We pointed out the patterns in window panes, the symmetry in the walls of our home. Noticing patterns in material that we wore on our bodies, on the shells of snails and on the backs of giraffes, we notated them. I found that God, the grand weaver, had stitched so much detail into his creations that it amazed my mind as I pointed them out for my children or vice versa.

The most amazing thing for me as I walked through this intentional journey was how God was filling in the blanks of my mis-educated life. I saw things that I never noticed before. It was almost as if God gave me children to stop me from living a dead life. My husband and my eyes of understanding the world were opening in a new way, as we taught our children about the world. Our worlds were broadening.

I noticed that one of our sons excitedly leaned toward mathematics, scientific discoveries, and orderly processes. He tinkered with everything. This one truly was scientific minded. I exposed him to things that encouraged this natural desire. He is the eldest and his leadership skills just seem to come naturally. Wouldn't you know that today he is a twice graduate, with an Engineering Associate from Piedmont Community College and an Engineering Bachelors from West Point Military College. Today he is an Officer in the United States Army.

I am writing this to you years later, so it brings me joy to look back at how God has weaved the tapestry that is our lives. This is profound for me, because my husband and I faced a lot of negative comments when we first started this journey. Some doubted me because of that upbringing that I spoke of earlier, and my husband because he took me as a readymade family. Yet God is able to use the weak vessels of this world to accomplish his will.

Another of our sons was definitely a social person. He attracted the attention of others pretty easily. He seemed to love talking to others, being with other people, and participating in group activities. He had a way with people that shown forth charisma. He leaned towards language and he loved to read. God gave him opportunities to lead others in Bible study classes. He was able to lead others through song, as a choir leader. As a Naval Academy Officer candidate, he was chosen to lead in various extracurricular activities. He has always exhibited defined leadership skills. Earlier on in his educational journey, I knew that he would do something that had to do with working with people. That son graduated with a bachelor's degree in Criminal Justice, and he is also an Officer in the United States Army.

My third son, oh, now *he was a handful*. Not as in giving us defiant troubles, but just his inquisitiveness. This son of ours was not a mathematics, scientific kind of guy. He is a business man to his heart, always trying to come up with ways to create income. Some of his ventures put us out of a few $100 dollars, but I thought it essential to help him to find his niche. Like his older brother, he was a self-motivated person. He didn't necessarily need a lot of people to approve of his venture capital ideas in order for him to try them. He tried breeding and selling worms which seemed to work for a while, until he left the worm bend outside and it rained. Then the next day, he thought if he left it in the sun that the sun would dry up all the rain from the soil. Well, you can just about figure out what happened to that business. Then, he decided to make ice cream to sell at the wine festivals where I was a vendor. Then he saw that there were already too many established ice cream vendors around, and he scrapped that venture. He crafted jewelry to sell at farmers markets. He purchased products at whole sale prices to resale online. This son also started a lawn care business that he runs still to this day over the summers. His work ethic is one that has gained him a tremendously good reputation in the neighborhood. He also, has worked as a video producer, helping to create various documentaries and short movies for various organizations in our surrounding cities. This son is in his junior year at Liberty University seeking a Business Major, and a minor in Cinematic Arts. Totally him.

Now for our baby, he is the firm stickler, the tradesman. I think that he is also a bit spoiled. I say that because he has taken it slow and steady. He is calm and laid back, trying to figure out which way to go. He tends to enjoy watching and assisting the people whom we have hired to come into our home to repair something. Upon our request, the tradesman enjoyed giving him a few lessons in their trade. He loved helping these guys when they worked in our home. He watches and assists his dad as he repairs our cars, or lawn mowers. He has also, taken advantage of the opportunity to learn from our neighbor, who happens to be a small engine technician. He has worked with timber home builders while learning their processes and technics. This son worked with a local lumberjack learning how to clear land. He has worked in the family business, learning how to detail brand new homes. He and his brother have run the lawn mowing business for a few years now. Yes, he is the one that attempts to repair the equipment when it breaks down. We have requested him to build different small sheds around the property and watched him complete them to our delight. So, it is no wonder that he wants to be in the business of buying and purchasing real estate and managing multiple businesses. He doesn't want to work them all, just buying and managing them. We can see that this is definitely an area where he excels and has always enjoyed.

During our journey to intentionally raise these boys, we have trusted and believed that Gods hands have been on our family. This guidance has helped my husband and I navigate through the maze of homeschooling our children. With His guidance we have tried to successfully move them towards the way that they have leaned. There were a lot of our desires instilled within their souls, but gentle enough that they were open and flexible. Oh, please know that there were many times where we bumped heads with our boys, but we have always been able to come to a conclusion that worked out for all of us.

Something that I noticed about the people in the intentional parenting examples listed above is this; No matter how much education, or how much money the parents had, it didn't seem to stop the results. These factors didn't weigh as heavily upon the conclusive results as did the pure love and tenacity of the parents. These two factors seemed to have played an extremely important role in shaping the future of the child. The people that I listed above excelled because they had parents to walk with them all the way until they succeeded.

As a parent, father or mother, you will have to give a lot. If you find yourself in the position where the bulk of the responsibility to homeschool and care for the kids falls on you, then you must be all out dedicated. I can't say this enough, but, you have to be all in. It is imperative for the success of your children's chances to obtain their goals.

Remember, the ultimate choice to homeschool will be made between you, and if you are a Christian, 'God'. Your children will not be very happy with you or their lives if they are deprived of their chances to go forward. I have lived to learn this with my boys, in the area of sports.

Unknowingly, we chose to move to a town that didn't offer many opportunities in sports for them once they past eighth grade. One of my sons thinks that this affected his skills in some sports. Luckily, he can appreciate all the many other opportunities he has enjoyed and doesn't dwell on our decision to move to the country. Not anymore that is.

I am saying all of this to impress upon you that you must cherish your role enough to prosper in it. Treat it as a season in your life to be used to shape and mold a future citizen of your country, an asset to the world, a future leader of the millennial to come. I cherished the time that I had with my boys, and I truly miss the days of rich relationship parenting. So, don't feel inferior, but trust in His abilities, do not lean to your OWN understanding.

Middle School and More

Speaking of being intentional, this time in the life of our oldest son was an eye opener for us. Not because our son was entering sixth grade, but because he was entering sixth grade classes and activities within our church. I think that this time marked us as being overbearing parents. It was at this level, that the kids going into sixth grade were entering youth groups, where they did lock-ins, retreats, and other various trips.

    As a parent, you will need to be extra intentional; your children are at the stage in life where they are branching out more into the world. They will come up under the influences of many other people and their ways of life. We understood that we had to ensure that our sons kept our way of life, our way of living. This may sound a little controlling, but we noticed a lot of kids in our church youth group, getting into things that were very inappropriate as well as disrespectful to others.

Intentional parenting must recognize these things and take actions to buffer them off. I know that my sixth-grade son was no angel, but I also knew what he had been exposed too. Up until the time that he was eligible to go, we had observed many disturbing behaviors from some of the kids involved in youth group. Nearly all the incidents happened with the children of the leaders of the group. This is what influenced our decision most of all not to allow our son to participate in those activities. This was mainly, due to the fact, that the leadership at the time was very liberal with their rules and regulations. We could see that some of the kids in the group had paired up as boyfriend and girlfriend.

There were certain girls in the group fighting over a boy. On a few occasions, we witnessed kids kissing and touching right in the sanctuary. On a certain day, I confronted two of the teenagers, and that didn't go over very well.

I remember the father, who happened to walk in on our talk, acting as if he wanted to bury his head in the sand.

That really jolted me into disbelief. I thought, "How can I allow this person to lead my child, when he doesn't have the power to put his own child in check?

This same leadership was always organizing outings for the kids or a church lock-in. I sometimes think that leadership like this is trying to find a way-out for their own hard-head children, trying to appease their need to socialize. As a homeschooling parent, being a part of this kind of group can become very tempting, but please use caution, you just might introduce your child to more rebellious peers than you would like to deal with. I do understand the importance of our children being around those that do not come from a home that is directed by Christian values. I believe our children need to be able to relate to others that might not know much about God. But we really have to guard them at this age, our children are so easily swayed.

So as long as the church kept the leadership it had for the youth, we made the decision to keep our kids away from youth group, and Awana. Yes, that meant that we had to diligently seek out extra activities for them to participate in while at the church. Well, I just advocated in the 'name of Jesus' on their behalf. It also helped that there were a lot of homeschooling families that felt the same need to protect their children from those kinds of influences while they were young. I approached certain ones in other leadership roles in the church family to get my son a place to serve and learn at the same time. The media room always needed help, so he shadowed the main guy learning the skill of running sound and the computer. My husband and I were ever so grateful to this man for taking him up under his coaching.

This was one way that our kids stayed occupied and served while in church. I was one of the leaders to work with the kids in the youth choir, so naturally all my sons were also in the choir. This was really an excellent choice for us, because they were learning true musicality. They were singing parts, which by the way is a dying skill in the modern church today. They were learning from people who truly loved God and music. They were able to sing in front of the congregation which helped them with speaking publicly. Because we homeschooled, my boys also participated in the band, which gave them plenty of opportunities to play in front of the church and sometimes with the accompaniment of the church's pianist.

Most of all, these boys learned to love serving in God's house.

We kept them so busy that they did not have time to miss something that they never had, especially the youth group. Don't misunderstand me; the boys had plenty of interactions with youth. My boys played on sports teams and swam with a team. These activities come with socializing built within them. We didn't mind socializing; we just wanted to insure the right kind and to provide leadership that was safe and firm.

Your priority as a parent, especially the mom, is to the child first, because she is the one with the child for the majority of the day. You are to guide the child through the maze of choices when he or she is too young and naive to choose wisely. It is a proven fact that children are unable to think logically enough to decide whether something is right or wrong for them, by looking into their own future. Some choices must be made by you as a parent, whether it makes you popular with your child or not. If you have a relationship built on trust and love, your child will come to understand that you are for their good. But you must do it out of love for their lives and be sure to convey that to their very fragile and tender hearts.

As a mother of all boys, I felt blessed. I couldn't believe that God had entrusted me with so many male lives. I thought for some moments, who am I to care for their lives? How in the heck can I raise these boys? I didn't know the first thing about family.

Yet, there was one thing I did know and understand. I knew that all children needed love, acceptance and protection. I did understand that when a child is young he or she is at the most vulnerable stage in life. I understood that there were people out there that would hurt them, all while smiling in my face. I knew this because it happened to me, and I was not protected, loved nor accepted. These experiences taught me not to be so trusting in everybody. I love socializing, and enjoying life with my kids, but I watched them like a mother eagle when they were young.

At this age, your child is going through some serious emotional and hormonal changes. This is the age when they are struggling with their perception of self. They are transitioning from being small little kids without a care in the world to suddenly seeing that the world isn't all about fairy tales that ends happily ever after. Their brains are changing, and their bodies are changing. They are developing their sexual selves and feelings that are natural but overpowering at times. This is so important. This is the time that you must know your child. Do not allow anyone or anything to become bigger in their lives than you are as the parent. Nothing should influence them more than your loving leadership. Your child's brain is trying to figure out who they are, and you do not want Satan giving them the answer.

My husband and I talked with our children on a regular basis. We always ate dinner together, laughing and talking as we did that routinely. This practice allowed us to see into our children's soul. We could help them understand harsh words that were said to them in passing. We could show them how to analyze a situation to find the reasoning behind it. We discovered that research proves that eating at least one meal together as a family really is a beneficial asset. Everyone involved is important and can be confirmed right at the dinner table. Your adolescent child really needs to be pulled in a little closer so that you can love on him or her just that much more.

Yes, be an ever-present force in your children's lives, they need to know you are there. You must know your children so well that you can attest to their character without hesitation. You must know them so well that you can help to identify their weakness and strength. Knowing each one in this way, will not only help you to guide them in the way that each should go, but you can help them to narrow their path to make the right choices for their future.

Remember homeschooling isn't just about academics, rather it is the perfect setting to teach your child life skills. Your child's education is so much more than books. They have to know about the world that they live in and how to function in it.

When I was a teenager, I can remember my grandmother hurting her shoulder one year, which meant that she couldn't do the things for us that she usually did. This is the time that she brought me under her wing to teach me how to cook, how to shop, how to bank, and how to deal with business people in the public. I was only middle school age, but because of her guidance, I was able to run my own apartment when the time came for it. I didn't have any fears about managing my own household.

Although I was not homeschooled, and I didn't have a mom or dad in the home, I did have a grandmother to school me about being a grown up. It was my grandmother that gave me the skills to care for myself as a single person. I do recognize that in a very profound way she did help me to better fit into my role as a mother.

High School Days

Now is the time to start chiseling away at the master piece that God is using you to mold through life. I said earlier that homeschooling isn't just about academics. No, it is not. As homeschooling parents, we must help our children to see the big picture about life. We need to transfer to them the idea that they will be responsible for themselves soon. You'd want to help them get to that time of responsibility smoothly and to arrive there with wisdom.

Isn't it funny how when you look back at your own life, you can see the profound times that someone conveyed a life lesson to you that stuck with you forever?

I have had a few of those times. I know that not all these incidents were meant as perfect life lessons at the time, yet some still managed to turn on a positive action within my spirit.

Like the time when my biological mother told me that my freshly painted lips looked like a bloody 'Explicit'. This was after I had asked how her red lipstick looked on my lips. Although, I am sure that she was not trying to seal a determined parental skill within my soul, let me tell you she absolutely did. That day, deep down within me, I understood that I would never say that kind of thing to my children.

This stayed with me throughout my season of hands on mothering. I realized that this is an extreme example, but this is what came to mind when I started writing about helping your children to see the big picture about life. As a young girl, I was extremely affected by my mother's words. These words hurt me, but molded me at the same time. So, I wanted to be intentional with my sons as I chose words to chisel away at their character development. I wanted my sons to be strong and wise.

With this focused attitude, my husband and I chose many activities to help our sons figure out which way they should head, as they pursued their future life career. Since they were big strapping young men now, one of the first things that my husband decided was that they needed to learn how to work outside the home. We didn't want our children to be 18 years old and not have any idea what it was like to work for someone else. We had trained them to work around the home and had taught them to help run our family business. Yet, we knew that they would need to experience functioning in a work environment.

Using these tactics helped our sons to see if they really wanted to pursue the many occupations that they were fantasizing about. We were always pushing them towards practical experience. You can believe that this is the optimum way for your child to know if he or she really wants to do a particular job.

With this goal in mind we moved forward. When our oldest son told us about his dream of being a veterinarian, I approached a friend of ours who was the head nurse at the local veterinarian hospital. She was also a homeschooling mom and loved the idea of training a fellow homeschooled child. Our son got a chance to work with all kinds of small animals that came into the hospital. He cared for the cages, transported the animals back and forth. He got a chance to assist with surgeries and recoveries.

It was a true hands on experience for him. He was working in the profession and receiving pay for his time, it was a definite plus.

During this period, we lived in the country, and I realized that he would need to learn about bigger farm animals. Also, my other sons were getting interested about horses, cows, sheep, goats and alpacas. So, we decided to join 4H groups. This exposed my oldest son to all of these different animals. The first group that we participated in was a horse 4h club. We soon discovered that it consisted mostly of girls, only one boy. We joined anyway. I figured that handling horses was a skill that they would need to use some day, and it was part of my mind set to teach as God taught many of His children. He helped them to become knowledgeable about as much as they could so that they could make wise choices, while preparing to serve him.

Although, deep down inside, I was really afraid of these huge creatures. But, I didn't let my boys know it. So, we participated in these groups for a few years. During this time, my oldest discovered that he was very allergic to horse hair. Every time it came time to groom these animals, he would nearly sneeze his head off. It was a debilitating time for him. Because, he couldn't control the sneezing, nor could he do anything else while the episodes lasted. Well, this and the fact that he did not like smelling like dogs when he got home, helped him to decide against being a veterinarian.

Oh well, at least he gained some valuable experience. Skills that he will always be able to use if needed, in his own life with pets. This was a real-life, hands on lesson for my son. A lesson that kept him from wasting many years and from wasting thousands of dollars, pursuing a degree in Veterinarian medicine.

One of our other sons thought that he might want to be a farmer. So, we kept up with the 4h groups. This time we joined one that handled, cows, sheep, goats and alpacas. My entire family helped out with this particular 4h group. This required us to care for over 50 heads of cattle. Wow! What an experience. Two of them were calves that the boys had to raise to participate in the 4H program.

The boys learned how to feed and water the cows. They had to groom the cows. They had to assist in dehorning and castrating the bulls. This was the hardest part for me. Seeing that blood squirting out all over the place, yuck! It didn't seem to bother the boys in the least bit.

We had to make sure that the cattle were kept warm and protected from the weather, by keeping the barn filled with clean dry straw. Since we had to work with them through a Virginia winter, it was most challenging, having to go through that. I nearly froze every time I would drive them to the farm. Yes, that's another thing; I had to be the driver, since my older sons were off doing other things and the remaining two didn't have their license yet.

Now this was one of those situations, where my sons were under the supervision of a more experienced farmer and one where I would never have left them alone with him. This person approached us when we first joined the 4H club. He offered us the opportunity to purchase our calves through him and the option to keep them on his land.

The tradeoff was we had to contribute by working the farm every day. I really did appreciate this opportunity and we did enjoy the challenge. Yet, he wasn't someone that I would have let, have alone time with any of my boys. My alert antennas came up when he would offer to drive them anywhere or to pick them up from our home.

This relationship stands out in my mind, because it turned out to be very shifty. So much so, that the 4H leadership where watching us very closely. I was unaware of this until the end. That's when the group leader made my husband and me aware of what this person was doing in our children's names. Yet, God gave me supernatural discernment during the entire year to keep a close grip on the boys during this time of learning.

Well, we successfully raised our two calves until they were both well over 2000 pounds. After the project was over, we had been exposed to the other animals just by participating in the program. We realized right away that pigs were off the list. My boys learned how to butcher chickens, pluck the feathers and gut them. They were given lessons on how to dress deer. From the skinning of them, to the butchering of the meat. Let me tell you, this was also totally gross for me. Yet, once again the boys seemed to like it. But as they got older the son that we kept this up for changed his mind about being a farmer.

But just think about the many skills that the boys were able to learn as they went through the hands-on process. These are skills that they will have for a life time. Yet it eliminated years of waste, trying to become something, only to find out that you hate it in the end. These kinds of experiences helped us as parents, to weed out feelings for a romanticized occupation, from the true ones.

Still, another one of our sons had aspiration towards the music ministry. Since he and his brothers all played various instruments and had sang in many choirs, he had developed a good ear for harmony. My husband and I took advantage of these skills by arranging for them to play on various occasions, in and out of church. This gave us a pretty good idea as to which one would enjoy this kind of performance and which one wouldn't. This particular son, would often take the role of worship leader and help to organize the songs that we were working on as a family.

Needless to say, I made sure that he was part of every musical opportunity that I became aware of in the church. Also, we wanted to expose him to music from many different angles, so we were able to get him involved in the local theater group. This is where he learned how to run their sound system, working on professional plays. This son played and sang on the church praise band.

Also, he and his older brother traveled with a local youth choir that went up and down the east coast to different churches performing. One summer, he and a group of other young people did a street music ministry that put him in front of various audiences.

I think that he really loved music and performance. Yet, this is not the area of study that he chose in the end when he went to college.

So, this is why I want to encourage you to seek out as many hands-on opportunities that you can for your child. So that you will know with more assurance which way to guide them when the time comes.

I thank God for the different avenues that he provided for these boys to find themselves. Homeschooling has been a good fit for us to help them on their way to adulthood.

To further tailor each boy's education, we noticed their different academic strength. Since, one of our sons enjoyed doing the higher math's and sciences, he seemingly had a natural mind for it, so we kept encouraging him to go forward. We also graduated him early from homeschool, so that he could enroll into the community college to take Geometry, Physics, and College English 111. In addition, we knew this would challenge him to be accountable to outside teachers. Our choice turned out to be a very good one for him, because he flourished there. I am so thankful for the prompting of the Holy Spirit, who helped me to know when to let go of my students. If we want to be successful, we must watch our children closely to direct them as we're guided by the Holy Spirits. This is not unlike the job of a guidance counselor in the public-school system. Yet, if directed by the Holy Spirit it is even better. So, you do not have to send your child to public school in order to get him more advanced classes. Our son was able to graduate high school early, and he earned an Engineering degree from the community college. You see, the same year that he would have officially graduated from public high school, he already had a college degrees. This method of tailored leadership really has worked out well for our children.

Our third son just went straight from homeschool to college enrolling in the Cinematic Arts program. This son really had a focused mindset as to what he wanted to do. So, while he was still doing high school work, I also found opportunities for him to get hands on practice in his career choice. He got into a local program and they gave him real jobs, working in the Cinematic Arts field. This gave him real live opportunity to create live projects with local professionals. People who were successful in the industry and willing to mentors young people. He saved up his money to purchase his own movie camera and we helped him to buy the other components needed. This was an exciting opportunity for him, which he was already profiting from. There were jobs that put him directly in front of the public as an interviewer/biographer. I am talking about jobs that paid him to produce real live footage for public viewing. A awesome benefit if this is where you want to work.

Our son received numerous scholarships to attend film classes, gaining knowledge about producing movies while still in homeschool.

He was even awarded a scholarship to attend a 17wk business course that taught him the process of starting a business and how to put together a business plan. The class was one that I also attended, it was no frivolous opportunity. It opened doors for me to get my products out into the public and into stores like Wholefoods Market.

The freedom aspect of homeschooling is something we appreciated. We knew that he would not have been able to benefit from these opportunities if he had been regulated by the restricted time of a public school schedule.

This son really had an education tailored toward the way that he leaned as he was growing into adulthood.

Still, another of our sons seemed to be so interested in the trades. He really seemed to enjoy anything that had to do with building construction. As I talked about in an earlier chapter, he was drawn to the work of the guys we hired to do work in our home. He just seemed to gravitate toward that kind of thing. So, with the professional tradesman permission, we allowed our son to assist them.

A lot of the time he was a gopher, but still picking up valuable skills and insight as he did the running. Of course, I went to work. Scouting out more opportunities for him to gain more hands-on experience. I contacted some friends and found a perfect situation for him to work with professional builders on Montpelier's historic site. This job immersed our son straight into the realness of building. He was learning building technics of the colonial days from a mater builder.

If you ever visit the museum and the home of James Madison at Montpelier, in Virginia.

You will see some of the buildings that he helped to reconstruct. This was truly a dual opportunity for him. As he learned the building process, he was also learning archeology. He had the privilege of assisting the head archeologist at Montpelier. Helping to unearth artifacts and to locate some of the old slave quarters, covered long ago by time. This rigorous, yet fun opportunity gained him 1 college credit from JMU, I was so shocked.

He hasn't finished high school yet but, he is well on his way toward his goal of being in project management. Which will more than likely have to do with building and the business management side of real estate. He is currently enrolled at the local community college taking some of the elective classes for a degree in business.

All our sons have been introduced to many career paths before ever graduating high school. Each have had jobs in many different environments, they've volunteered in places that exposed them to varying career choices. They have had chances to work with professionals in many areas. Such as sculpting, with the master sculptor Thomas Marsh at the

Orange Art center. He also taught them drawing, and painting. All the boys had art lessons with him. The two oldest assisted Mr. Marsh in the restoration of the James Madison museum in Orange, Virginia. Which was written about in the local newspaper.

They had a few opportunities to work with professionals at the local theater to put on a few productions of plays. The two oldest worked on production side. One learned how to operate the lighting system and the other son ran the sound system. They learned a very complex operation and did well enough to be offered chances to work on three professional plays. This allowed them to learn the behinds the scene parts of production. Which was another knowledge gaining experience for the son who went into Cinematic Arts. He and his younger brother acted in two of the plays. Guess who the den mother was! Yes, me!

    There was another time when two of our sons worked with a professional logger, learning how to clear land. This was a valuable experience for both, but especially for the son that's interested in construction and building.

These are just some ways that we have helped our sons to narrow their focus toward a career path. The fact that we homeschooled helped us to tailor their education toward each individuals interest. Also, this way of educating them, enabled us to have all boys participate in the hand on activity if they so desired.

In addition to the various apprenticeship opportunities, each son have worked for companies that they chose. Two of the boys were clerks at Foodlion groceries store. While another worked at the same old grind coffee shop, and at the community college he attended. Still, another son actually got the chance to work for a winery. He learned how to tend to the grapes in the vineyard and assisted in the wine making. We wanted them to not just excel in academics, but to understand what it would be like living in the real world. Working and living on their own.

College

Now we have walked through the steps of training our sons in lives' many mind fields of choices. Attempting to reinforce the natural abilities within them, we guided them toward the best fit for each oneself. We all have this ability, but most of us do not learn to tap into it until we are much older.

Even so, we have come to the time where they must choose. You know, I believe because we had given them the chance to do so many things while they were still home, it made the transition easy. All of the above opportunities really did ease the finale choice for them at the end of the homeschool days.

Even if they hadn't chosen college, I know the working skills that they picked up during the school days, provided them with a hardy dosage of reality about what's required in adulthood. All the boys applied for jobs and worked in environments where strangers were their bosses. Not all their employment opportunities came from our friends and family. As I said earlier, two of our sons worked for the Food lion corporation. Another worked with a home builder. One worked as a lifeguard and swim coach for a fitness center. His boss didn't want him to leave, because he was such a reliable employee.

Their work ethic and responsible attitude helped them to build very good reputations around the community. This is something that they worked hard to achieve. My husband and I often received grateful praises and accolades about our parenting because of their work ethics.

Imagine that, our children's bosses giving us praises about how we raised our sons. Without fail, each boss told us that our sons were the best workers they had and wanted to know when our other two would be old enough to work. This was not so much a testament to our ability as parents, but directly related to our persistent goal to teach our sons responsibility. My husband worked very hard to provide for his children and they knew that he was there for them and me. We tried hard to impress upon them that they owed responsible character to the world and to their God.

Each son arrived at this point with a pretty good idea as to which direction he wanted to go. Now all we had to do was help each one sift through the many options presented them. We helped them to pursue and apply to all college options that fit their choices.

To prepare our first son, we attempted to obtain every credential that we thought that he might need. My husband and I did this particularly, because he was our first homeschooled graduate. We made him take all known test to equip him for college entrance and higher education. He took the GED tests. We awarded a homeschool diploma through HEAV (Home Educators Association of Virginia). He was the class of 2010 where he walked across stage with the other 200 plus graduates. We enlisted the help of a good friend from our church, to take our son through rigorous exercises in preparation for the SAT and ACT tests. Dr. Dennis Rowe drilled him for many months to get him ready. We had to pay for our son to take the ACT and the SAT as many times as he needed, in order to get his scores where they had to be. We helped pay for his classes at the local community college where he graduated with an Associates in Engineering. Attempting to cover all the bases with this one, we probably went a little bit over board. But, we didn't want to end up regretting that we had not provided all the right tools. We wanted to give him everything he needed for him to enter any college of his choice. He would have to be the testament for our choice to homeschool.

So, armed with outstanding SAT and ACT scores, an Associates in Engineering, and a resume three pages long, our first homeschooled son/student/graduate, applied to West Point Military Academy. He received a nomination from Senator Eric Cantor and was accepted to the West Point Academy Preparatory school.

At the same time, our second son submitted his application to the Naval Academy and he was accepted. Wow! We were absolutely floored. Praising God, we realized that this was a direct result of the homeschooling preparatory choices we had made for our sons. We came to this conclusion because our second son had not gone to community college during high school. He was accepted straight out of high school, this convinced us of that fact. We had exposed each of them to many volunteer opportunities as well as work opportunities; coupled with the four years of English, Math and 2 years of Foreign Language. Their resumes were very impressive for high school students. Senator Cantor's personal secretary told us so on the phone. He appointed both of our sons, one to the West Point Academy and one to the Naval Academy.

This is something that brings me satisfaction and pride, considering from whence we started. I, a girl from the streets of San Francisco, the Fillmore district, would have never thought that I would be sitting here writing about sons that I helped to educate.

I had not taught in the normal way of educating someone. The only way that I was used to and had witness all of my life. No, our journey was in a very hands-on sense. I truly believe that God pulled me out of this long line of normal and expected family behavior concerning the job of raising children.

He put me on a specific path. I don't know why He blessed me with the privilege of raising my own children from infant to adulthood, and I know that this is not unique to the world, but it is to my world.

I've never had anyone from my blood family that had done this homeschool thing. Actually, it saddens me to say, in my immediate family, a precious few have actually raised their own children. To this day, I wonder what happened to my mother's side that so corrupted the natural instinct to parent. I do realize that as African American people, we had to fight against the evils of being torn apart from one another without any regard for our lineage. But this lack of emotional ties comes from something much deeper. Yet, I am so grateful to see that some of my younger relatives are firming up against the rifts that has torn our family apart. They are beginning to embrace the naturalness of parenting their own children. They are being their children's protectors, being their all and all during the young and vulnerable.

Our third son is about to start his third year at Liberty university, as a Business major with a minor in Cinematic Arts. He reordered the focus of his degree after his second year. We are pleased to say that he is doing very well - and is maturing into a very capable young man.

This is the last year that we will homeschool our youngest son. He is in his senior year, and it already feels as if he is out of the house. He is dual enrolled at community college and runs his lawn business on his off days. This son is considering a degree in business from a real estate prospective.

My point of sharing this with you is not to brag or pat myself on the back. It is because I want to help others who might be where I was when I first started having babies. Clueless as to what motherhood was all about. I had to come into my role as a mother; I had to learn a way to parent. I didn't have deep seeded parental know-how within me. Yet, I was successful at parenting despite my upbringing, my lack of moral teaching, my absent father, my exposure to and my embracing of everything sinful and evil.

I give all glory to God and His ability to take the weak, broken, losers of this world and using them as vessels to accomplish his work.

Isaiah 49:15 (NKJV) "Can a woman forget her nursing child, And not have compassion on the son of her womb? Surely they may forget, Yet I will not forget you.

Although not an exhaustive list, the following books are some of the core resources that we have used throughout the years of homeschooling our 4 sons.

Horizon & Lifepacs books

These were our very first choices for math and language when we were starting out and the kids were young.

Abeka books

These turned out to be our core curriculum for language, math, science, & history, once our children hit 4th grade.

Saxon Math- used only when I thought someone needed a different method on comprehending a math concept.

Math -u- See- The books and especially the manipulative. This is an excellent hands-on curriculum set to help the kinesthetic learner grasp harder concepts.

www.ingramcontent.com/pod-product-compliance
Lightning Source LLC
LaVergne TN
LVHW051044080426
835508LV00019B/1701